THE DESTRUCTION of TROY

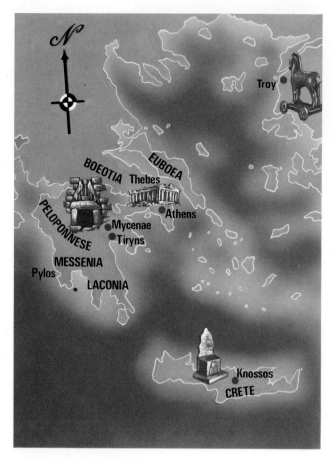

Endpaper: The Trojan prince Aeneas flees from burning Troy, with his aged father Anchises on his back and his small son Ascanias (see page 37).

Photographs by courtesy of Popperfoto (page 7, Schliemann), the British Museum (page 7, Madam Schliemann) and Barnaby's Picture Library (page 42, Mycenae, page 45, the Acropolis).

Map: Roland Berry

Published in the United States by Rand McNally and Company 1977

Designed and produced by Intercontinental Book Productions

Contents

IN SEARCH OF LOST WORLDS

THE DESTRUCTION of TROY

Written by Robert Wilson

Illustrated by Michael Codd and Roland Berry

Rand McNally & Company

Chicago   New York   San Francisco

I Schliemann's excavations
Gold at Troy

In July 1873, a German archaeologist, Heinrich Schliemann, and his beautiful young wife Sophia discovered a great hoard of gold at Hissarlik in Turkey near the shores of the Aegean Sea. Hissarlik is thought to be the site of ancient Troy, the city which 3000 years ago was the home of mighty heroes and warriors, a place with fine palaces and temples. Once it was so powerful that it took the ancient Greeks ten years to conquer its people, the Trojans, and burn down the city in one of the most famous wars in history. Now it is just a mound, overgrown with thorny scrub.

Schliemann had been excavating at Troy for four months and was just about to pack up and finish his work there. Then, on the morning of May 30, 1873, while working near the huge fortification walls, he suddenly noticed a glint of metal among the rubble. Immediately he sensed that he was very near the treasure. Since he knew that the Turkish government would try to claim it and feared that his workmen would try to steal it, he told his wife to call out to all the laborers on the site that it was his birthday, so everyone must take the day off and go home. Soon the whole site was deserted except for Schliemann and his wife. It is said that she brought an enormous red shawl, which she laid on the ground, and then watched breathlessly as her husband dug out the treasure with his pocket knife and poured it onto the shawl. Schliemann was convinced that the treasure he had discovered was none other than that of King Priam, the last ruler of Troy. That night it was taken to a friend's house some distance away and a few days later it was smuggled out of Troy into Greece.

The treasure included a copper shield and cauldron, a silver case, a gold bottle, two gold cups, daggers, knife blades, lance heads, and three large silver vases; but the most amazing part of the find was two gold diadems. These strange and beautiful headdresses were made of golden leaves, rings with long tassels, chains to hang at the side of the face, and necklaces of many golden chains. In addition, more than fifty gold earrings were found and more than 8000 gold rings and buttons. The gold gleamed with a wonderful glowing reddish color. Nothing like this had been seen before: it was the most exciting archaeological find ever made.

Schliemann photographed the treasure and sent an account of the discovery to almost every

Heinrich Schliemann and (above) his wife Sophia, who is wearing a golden diadem of ancient Troy.

learned society in Europe. The Turkish government was beside itself with rage at losing that priceless part of its heritage, and the Greeks were unable to trace it in their own land. It was assumed that Sophia Schliemann, herself a Greek, had arranged for it to be hidden by members of her own family.

Schliemann's dream

Heinrich Schliemann was born in 1822 in a little village in Mecklenburg in Germany. Throughout his childhood his father, the village pastor, told him legends and stories of ghosts and buried treasure. Their home was surrounded by ghosts. Just outside the parsonage wall was a pond where a maiden was believed to rise each midnight with a silver bowl in her hands, and a kilometer away stood a mound where a child had been buried in a golden cradle. These stories fascinated the young Heinrich, but for him, none was as fascinating as the story of ancient Troy. On Christmas Day, 1829, he was given a present which was to fire his imagination and change the whole course of his life. As he opened it, Ludwig Jerrer's *Illustrated History of the World*, his eyes fell on a wonderful picture. It showed Troy in flames and Aeneas, plumed and helmeted, striding through the smoke with his old father on his back and his son by his side. Heinrich was sure that the artist must have seen the city to have drawn it so powerfully, although his father told him that Troy had been completely destroyed.

Heinrich made a secret vow that one day he would find the walls and towers of Troy shown in the picture. To this end, he began to learn all he could about the ancient Greeks and Trojans.

Homer and the story of the Trojan war

Much of what Heinrich came to know about these heroic people is contained in two long poems, the *Iliad* and the *Odyssey*, which were written down in the eighth century B.C. by the great Greek poet Homer. Little is known about him. According to legend, he was a blind bard, who sang his tales in the courts of the states of Greece, accompanying himself on his lyre, or small harp. Very probably a number of wandering minstrels had repeated these stories over the generations without ever writing them down. It is possible that more than one poet wrote the *Iliad* and the *Odyssey*, gathering together tales of past heroes to create the epic poems that we know today.

These poems and other Greek legends describe the great war between the Greeks (or Achaeans, as Homer calls them) and the people of Troy, or Ilion, thought to have taken place in the eleventh century B.C., over 3000 years ago. The story goes like this . . .

Paris was the son of Priam, the King of Troy. He was handsome and brave and a very fair judge of all things. Because of his good judgment, Zeus, the lord of all the gods, ordered Paris to decide which of the three goddesses, Hera, Athena, and Aphrodite, was the most beautiful. They appeared to him in a dream and he chose Aphrodite, who had promised him that, if she won the contest, then the beautiful Helen would be his bride. Now Helen was already the wife of Menelaus, the King of Sparta in Greece. After Paris had sailed from Troy to Sparta and carried off Helen, Menelaus went to Agamemnon, the imperial overlord of Greece, and asked him to wage war against Troy. So the Trojan war began, and the gods and goddesses ranged themselves either on the side of Greece or of Troy and helped mortal men to perform great deeds. Hera and

Athena were naturally annoyed that Paris had not chosen them and so they turned against the Trojans, but Aphrodite gave all the help she could to Paris and the Trojan cause.

King Agamemnon summoned all the princes of Greece to join forces with him against Priam of Troy. A vast army was assembled, and a fleet of ships built, and the Greeks landed near Troy. They set up camp on the shore beside their ships, and there they remained for ten years without bringing the conflict to a conclusion. Some successful raids resulted in Trojan towns being captured and looted. These raids were led by Achilles, the bravest and most dashing of the Greek princes. But, as the months and the years passed, the Greeks became weary and disagreement broke out between Achilles and Agamemnon. Achilles refused to fight and, while he – the most feared of the Greek warriors – sulked alone in his tent, Hector, Prince of Troy, led his forces with such good effect that the Greeks were forced back to the very edge of the sea. In a fierce battle most of their leaders were wounded and their ships set on fire. At last, Patroclus, the closest and most dearly loved friend of Achilles, led his troops into battle and was killed by Hector. When Achilles heard the news, he was overcome by terrible sorrow and a fearsome anger, and he vowed that he would avenge the death of Patroclus and kill Hector. During that night the god Hephaestus forged a new armor for Achilles and on the following day he and Hector met in deadly combat. Hector was slain and Achilles, in his desperate desire for revenge, stripped the dead hero naked, pierced his feet, and tied his body to the back of his chariot. Then he drove in triumph, around and around Troy, dragging the mangled corpse behind him.

That event is one of the most famous of all the stories of the Trojan war. Stories such as this convinced the young Heinrich Schliemann that the remains of a great and powerful civilization were waiting to be found in Greece and Turkey, and it is to the tale of his discoveries that we now turn.

Achilles in triumph dragging Hector's corpse around the walls of Troy.

The treasure-seeker

Heinrich Schliemann's own story is almost as amazing as those of the ancient heroes that inspired him. When he was fourteen, his family fell on hard times. His father had been dismissed from his post as pastor, and so, in 1836, Heinrich went to work in a grocer's shop. For the next five years he lived the life of a slave, running errands, carrying heavy casks and crates and serving customers. He earned very little money and was desperately tired and wretched. He grew pale and weak and it seemed that he would die surrounded by packages of herrings, bottles of potato whisky, and whale-oil candles. Yet all this time, he was dreaming of wealth – vast wealth, gold and treasure: he needed only a push to send him out into the world to seek his fortune. Eventually, in a strange way, the "push" came.

One night a drunken miller lurched into the shop. He stood, swaying slightly in the light of the oil lamps, and started to recite poetry in a language that was mysterious and beautiful but unknown to Heinrich. It was ancient Greek, the poetry of Homer, and it struck a deep chord in Heinrich's heart. Tears flowed down his cheeks as he listened. He gave the miller three glasses of potato whisky, even though it cost him all the money he had, and he asked the man to repeat the lines again and again. Soon after this event, Heinrich borrowed a small amount of money from his uncle and went to Hamburg, where he boarded a sailing ship bound for South America. Less than a week after they had set sail, a violent storm came up in the North Sea. While the waves pounded the ship and the rain poured down on it, Heinrich tied himself to a bench and began learning Spanish! Around midnight, on the fourth day after they had left Hamburg, an enormous wave smashed all the portholes, flooding the cabins. The ship lurched violently. Heinrich sprang out of his bunk and, unable to find his clothes, rushed up onto the deck stark naked. It was fortunate that he did so, for almost immediately the ship went down. When he rose to the surface, he saw an empty cask floating near him. He remained in the icy, dark waters, clinging to the floating cask, until he was rescued the next morning.

The incident was typical of Heinrich's life, full of drama and narrow escapes, but always with a streak of good luck that enabled him to survive. In the 1840s he was in Amsterdam working for a firm of merchants and, within two years, learning to speak and write fluently no less than six languages. A letter arrived from Russia, but no one in the Dutch firm could speak Russian. Heinrich learned Russian within six weeks, answered the

The young Schliemann, working as an assistant in a grocer's shop, hears a drunken miller reciting Homer.

letter, and became so useful to the firm that he was soon sent to St. Petersburg as its agent in Russia. There he set about amassing his first fortune. He had an amazing business sense and never missed an opportunity to add to his wealth. By the time he was twenty-eight he was recognized as one of the great merchant princes of St. Petersburg. He worked every minute of the day to increase his business, and mixed as an equal with the wealthiest people in the land.

Always restless, even this did not satisfy him, so when he learned that his younger brother had made a fortune mining gold in the newly discovered California gold fields, he went to America. On June 4, 1851, he was in San Francisco in conference with the agents of Messrs. Rothschild and other businessmen, making preparations to set himself up as a buyer of gold dust in the tiny gold-rush town of Sacramento. That night, asleep in his hotel room after a tiring day, he was suddenly woken by screams and shouts of panic. The smell of smoke was in his nostrils and the sky was lit up by flames. He dressed hurriedly and rushed out to see his hotel melting in the flames minutes after he had left it. For the second time, it seemed that the gods were protecting him just as they had protected the heroes of ancient times.

He stayed in Sacramento for only nine months and in that short time made his second great fortune, nearly half a million dollars. Few, even in those feverish days of the gold rush, made money as swiftly as he. But it was a terrible time. He lived in constant fear of being robbed. Also, he

Schliemann escapes drowning by clinging to a floating cask in the bitterly cold waters of the North Sea.

caught the deadly yellow fever, and for days he lay on his back, vomiting and raving like a madman, his body covered with yellow spots. When he miraculously recovered from his third attack of fever, he made his way back to Europe.

In St. Petersburg again, he married a Russian woman and lived once more the life of a merchant prince. The Crimean War broke out in 1854, and in that time of general ruin, he succeeded in vastly increasing his wealth by trading in supplies for the army. By the end of 1855 he was worth a million dollars and his fortune continued to grow. But he was not happy. He traveled restlessly all over the world and always, at the back of his mind, was the thought of the lost civilization described by Homer. By 1868 he had learned classical Greek and thoroughly studied all the Greek legends. He became even more obsessed with the idea of archaeological discovery, and in that year he went to Greece and began digging.

However, Heinrich realized he had overlooked one requirement: he needed a wife who could support him in his work. He went to America to divorce his first wife, then wrote to a friend in Athens asking him to send him some photographs of beautiful young Greek girls. Among the pictures was one of a pretty, dark-haired girl called Sophia. When they met, Heinrich asked her to recite some Homer. She did so perfectly and he married her.

11

Schliemann at Troy

Heinrich Schliemann was the first person to carry out any serious excavations on the low hill called Hissarlik, which was supposed to be the site of Troy. It was an unexciting place, windswept and desolate, so lacking in mystery that some scholars had refused to believe that the palaces and towers of ancient Troy had ever been there. Some people thought that the steeper and more romantic looking hill near Bunarbashi, 4.8 miles (8 kilometers) to the south, was more likely to have been the site of the old city. The map shows, however, just how important such a site must have been. To the east lies Asia, to the west, Europe, and nearby is the narrow sea passage of the Hellespont, now called the Dardanelles. This was the point where the ancient trading route from Asia into Europe approached the shortest sea crossing. Troy would have been well placed to control that trading route, near the sea yet not so close that it could be surprised by a sudden attack. But, in 1870, there seem to have been only two people, an English-man – Frank Calvert, who had carried out a very small excavation at Hissarlik – and Schliemann, who believed firmly that Troy was a real city, and its walls, palaces, and treasure lay buried in the mound at Hissarlik.

Nowadays, archaeology is a specialized occupation requiring scientific methods of excavation and documentation. The diggers work slowly with a brush and small trowel, gradually uncovering every tiny object and recording it. But Schliemann was the first "modern" archaeologist and a man who did everything with great energy and speed. He cut a giant shelf out of the north side of the mound, 234 feet (71 meters) wide and 29.7 feet (9 meters) deep. When he realized he could hardly search the whole site in this way, he dug a great north to south trench over 19.8 feet (6 meters) wide. To begin with he had eighty laborers, but he soon doubled that number. He imported picks, spades, and wheelbarrows from England, and he stood over the workmen with a pistol in his belt and a riding whip in his hand. Living conditions in Hissarlik were very primitive so Schliemann built a wooden house on the

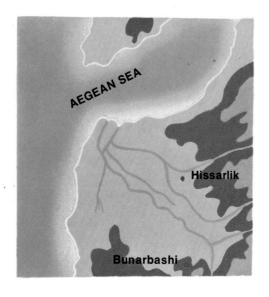

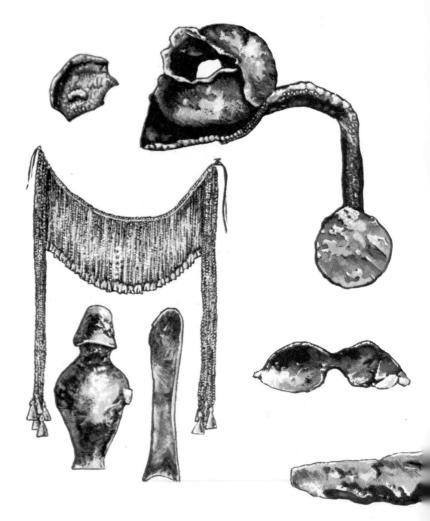

site for Sophia and him. There they lived and worked, inspired by the dream of Troy.

At first he found relatively little – some foundations, evidence that buildings had been burned and a gold coin which bore the inscription "Hector Ilieon" ("Hector of Troy"). But in 1872, at the southern end of his great trench, he came across what could only be city walls, built of large stones. There was a well-preserved entrance approached by a paved ramp, and Schliemann believed this was the Scaean Gate mentioned by Homer. Nearby were the remains of a great building which he thought must have been Priam's palace, and it was here that he found the treasure.

Schliemann's trench had cut a great slice out of the mound and, looking along the face of that slice, he was able to see that the mound had been built up from a number of layers. A city had been built. It had decayed in the course of time or been burned, and then more people had come along and built a new city on the remains of the old. This had happened many times. Schliemann saw clearly that there had been at least four main stages of prehistoric settlement on the site. Later archaeologists, engaged in more detailed excavations, have shown that at least eight Troys existed one after the other. The great walls that he found belonged to the second city, and the discoveries that he made near the walls showed that a civilization had existed in Troy in prehistoric times. Schliemann had proved that the legends of Homer and the Greeks were at least based on historical fact.

Schliemann smuggled the treasure out of Turkey within a few days of the discovery, and although the Turks insisted that he had promised to give half of anything he discovered to the Turkish government, he refused to say where the treasure was. Not surprisingly, the Turks immediately withdrew his permit to continue excavating at Troy, and so he turned his attention to Mycenae on the Greek mainland.

Gold objects found by Schliemann at Troy. The entire find has since disappeared. The map shows the relative positions of Hissarlik, the real Troy, and Bunarbashi.

13

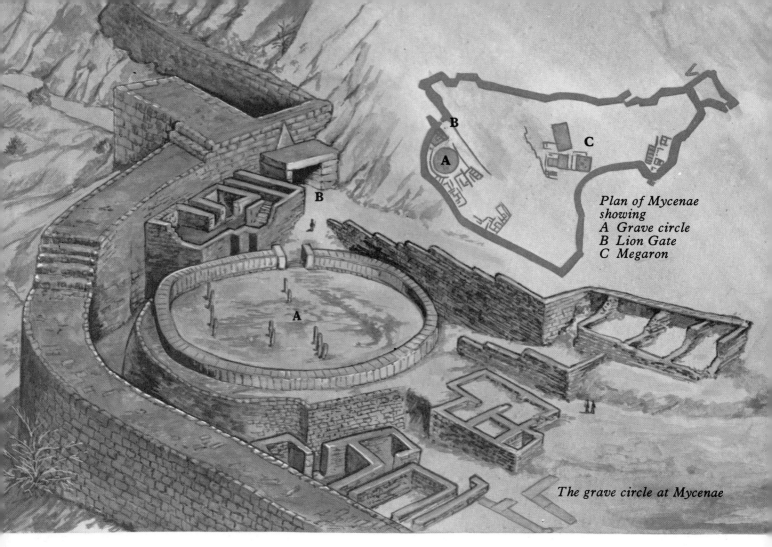

Plan of Mycenae
showing
A Grave circle
B Lion Gate
C Megaron

The grave circle at Mycenae

The treasure of the Mycenaean tombs

Mycenae was the obvious place to excavate. Many legends were attached to the city, most of them concerned with tragedy and bloodshed. The most famous was of Agamemnon, the powerful king of Mycenae and overlord of Greece, who led the Greeks in the war against Troy. During the ten long years that he was fighting at Troy, his wife, Clytemnestra, took a lover, Aegisthus. When Agamemnon's return was reported, the guilty lovers made desperate plans. On his arrival in Mycenae a great banquet was served. Afterwards, in a nearby bathroom, he was brutally murdered by his wife and her lover. This was the fulfilment of the curse on the family of Agamemnon's father, Atreus. To the later Greeks, it was as mighty a tragedy as the fall of Troy. Schliemann hoped to find the graves of Agamemnon and his family.

Even today Mycenae is a forbidding place. It stands on a hill commanding the plain of Argos, and behind it loom two great mountains. Wolves can be heard howling in the foothills. Here, in about 1700 B.C., an unknown but powerful king must have built gigantic ramparts around an even older city. The stones that were used were so large that later men believed that the walls had been built by giants, the Cyclopes, invited over from Asia Minor for the work. A paved highway ran up to the entrance gate, a massive stone structure on the top of which stood two carved lions facing each other. The Lion Gate is still the most dominant feature of Mycenae. Through the Lion Gate is a circular area which, when Schliemann arrived, was covered with the rubble and rubbish of the centuries. Beyond that lay tumbled, overgrown ruins. In his imagination Schliemann saw Mycenae as it had once been, a large and powerful city, with broad streets and fine palaces, and he remembered that Homer had spoken of the city as being "rich in gold." At Troy, Schliemann had found the treasure just inside the city walls, and instinct told him that here, in Mycenae, he should dig in the circular area near the Lion Gate.

Within a few months, Schliemann had uncovered a strange double ring of upright stone slabs 3.3 feet (1 meter) high enclosing a circle about 85.8 feet (26 meters) across. This area was thought to be the *agora*, the place of assembly where the city elders gathered for debate. As he dug down, Schliemann came across some gravestones carved with spirals and with pictures of warriors driving chariots or fighting with wild beasts. Later it was clear that these stones were markers for graves which had been cut in the soft rock several meters below. He also found a solitary gold button near the tombstones. Such discoveries strengthened Schliemann's hope.

But, perhaps because he wanted to put off the climax for a while, Schliemann turned his attention away from the grave circle and excavated what he believed to be the royal palace nearby. The first finds were not very exciting: scraps of pottery, little figures of goddesses painted red, axes, and hatchets. The most important discovery was a vase, about 12 inches (30 centimeters) high, on which an ancient artist had painted soldiers marching off to war. The colors are dark red on a pale yellow background and here, for the first time, men were able to see what the soldiers who fought at Troy looked like.

The months went on and little had been discovered apart from the gravestones and the vase. In the burning Greek sun, Schliemann worked all the hours of daylight while clouds of dust constantly swept over Mycenae. He was irritable and unwell and always quarreling with the Greek officials, who watched his every move in case he should steal any treasures he found, as he had done at Troy. But there was no treasure yet, and

The Lion Gate

The mask of "Agamemnon"

the distinguished visitors who came to see his work listened without belief to his boasts of finding the treasures of Agamemnon.

Summer ended and the rains came, but the work went on. At last, in the middle of October, Schliemann discovered a tomb cut into the rock about 15 feet (4.5 meters) below the surface of the agora. He dug a little further south towards the center of the circle and there, beneath a layer of pebbles, lay three bodies thickly covered with clay. Through the clay shone the gleam of gold. Too nervous to touch the bodies himself, he watched in mounting excitement as Sophia, crouching down in the hollow, carefully removed the clay from the bodies. Underneath were diadems made from thin sheets of gold decorated with circles and fourteen gold crosses.

This was the first of five graves found within the circle, each containing treasure. There were nineteen bodies in all, including those of three women and two children. Over the faces of some of the men were beautiful masks of thin gold; the women wore golden crowns or diadems, and their bodies were covered with many ornaments of thin gold which must once have been fastened to their clothes. Besides personal ornaments, there were cups and goblets of gold and silver and a wonderful silver vessel in the form of a bull's head, with horns of gold and a gold rosette on the forehead. In the last grave, Schliemann found what he believed was the greatest treasure of all. On a well-preserved body of a man about thirty-five years old lay a gold mask whose features resembled the pictures of Agamemnon that he had formed in his own mind many years before.

Further discoveries in the Aegean

For Schliemann, the graves that he had found in that circular area within the city walls of Mycenae were surely the graves of Agamemnon and his companions. To the day he died, he believed that he had looked on the face of the great king who had led the forces of Greece against Troy. Was he right? Alas, no! If we believe that Agamemnon was a real person, then he must have lived about 1180 B.C., which is the date that scholars give for the great war in which Troy was destroyed.

Since Schliemann's time, archaeologists have proved that Troy was indeed destroyed about that date. But they have also shown that the graves dug deep beneath that circular space, and now known as "shaft graves," were dug much earlier than the Trojan war, roughly between 1600 and 1500 B.C. Hundreds of discoveries on various sites in Greece and the nearby lands have enabled scholars to develop a way of dating the objects found in a sequence. This has been done mainly by studying the pottery found at different levels in a site. The pottery found near the surface must have been used by the more recent inhabitants of the site, and that found at the greatest depth must have belonged to the earliest settlers.

Schliemann's mistake was actually revealed by his brilliant young assistant, Professor Dörpfeld, who carried on working at Mycenae after Schliemann had left. Schliemann firmly believed that all the bodies in the graves had been buried at the same time because, he argued, it would have been impossible to dig down through the earth above to introduce a later burial without disturbing those already lying there. That seemed sensible enough, but Dörpfeld continued to wonder about two mysteries connected with the shaft graves. First, there had been strange slate slabs lying at odd angles over the bodies, and then there was the mystery of the little boxes of strong sheet copper which Schliemann had found in certain of the graves. They were filled with wood and fastened all around with a number of strong copper nails. He thought they might have been headrests, but no one really knew. They were sent to the museum in Athens with the other treasure.

Years later, Dörpfeld examined these little boxes carefully. He realized they were the ends of beams. At once he knew how the shaft graves had been used. Originally those slate slabs had covered the graves, high above the bodies at the surface level of the earth. The slabs had been supported on timbers, and the ends of the timbers resting on the ground had been strengthened by

copper coverings – Schliemann's "boxes." Each grave must have had a family vault in which it was quite possible for a newly dead prince to be buried without disturbing his father or grandfather. Burials in these vaults had extended over a century before 1500 B.C. Certainly they were kings and princes, the bodies that Schliemann found, but to Agamemnon they would have seemed as ancient as the Elizabethans do to us.

Eight years after his discoveries at Mycenae, Schliemann was again leading a massive excavation, this time at Tiryns, 9.6 miles (16 kilometers) to the south of Mycenae. It stands on flat land, surrounded by a level plain, and from a distance it looks like a great battleship, long, and low, and gray. It was not to yield the exciting treasures that Schliemann had discovered at Troy and Mycenae, but it was to tell him far more of how the ancient heroes of Homer's world had lived. It was also to give him further proof that a civilization had indeed existed in prehistoric Greece which was remarkably like that of which Homer wrote. For Schliemann here uncovered, with the help of seventy workmen, forty English wheelbarrows, twenty large iron crowbars, and masses of other

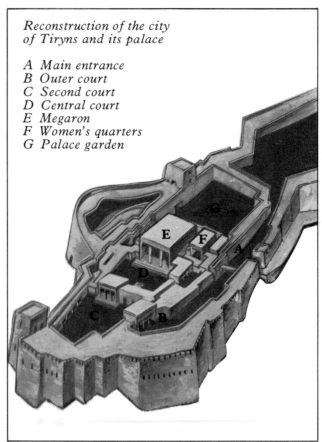

Reconstruction of the city of Tiryns and its palace

A *Main entrance*
B *Outer court*
C *Second court*
D *Central court*
E *Megaron*
F *Women's quarters*
G *Palace garden*

equipment, the clear ground plan of a city and palace. It had been lived in during the eleventh century before Christ. That was the time of the Trojan war, and it is easy to imagine Agamemnon living and ruling at Mycenae just to the north. Indeed, the palace of Tiryns is so similar to the palace that Homer describes in the *Odyssey* that he may well have had it in mind when he described the home of Odysseus in Ithaca.

A visitor to Tiryns would have come up the ramp to the entrance, which was defended by a tower. The visitor could have been one of the farmers or merchants who lived outside the walls, perhaps seeking protection within the city because of the danger of a raid. The large oval area has walls 19.8 feet (6 meters) thick and could accommodate not only the people who lived in the region around Tiryns but also their cattle and other animals. If the visitor had been important, and had come to see the king, he would have turned left inside the gate and driven in his light chariot through the outer court into a second court. This was surrounded by colonnades or galleries. Cattle were kept in this court for sacrificing at feasts. Our important visitor would have left his chariot and been led into the central court of the city. In front of him he would have seen the *megaron*, or men's hall, and to the right the women's quarters with its own hall. He would have been taken through the pillared porch of the vestibule and into the megaron where the king would have greeted him from his high seat.

Tiryns showed that people living in the fortress cities of Greece in the eleventh century before Christ lived in refined and civilized surroundings. They were a warlike people but they had spacious, airy palaces whose walls were covered with pictures painted on plaster – frescoes.

In 1878, just after Schliemann's discoveries at Mycenae, a Greek excavated at Knossos on the island of Crete. Among his finds were small fragments of pottery and an insignificant little clay tablet inscribed in an unknown script. This dig soon attracted the attention of scholars, for it was realized that the pottery, decorated in a glossy paint which varied in color from red to brown to black, was very close to what was known from Mycenae. Schliemann was certain that here was another great palace of the same date as Mycenae and Troy, and he wanted to excavate the site himself. But there were difficulties in buying the ground, and the excavation of Knossos was to fall to an Englishman, Sir Arthur Evans, who, between 1900 and 1905, unearthed an enormous palace on the site.

Unlike Mycenae and Tiryns, Knossos had

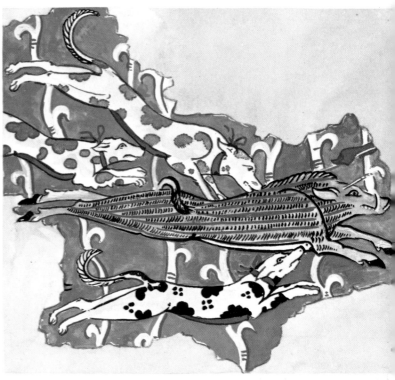

Fresco from Tiryns of a wounded boar being pursued by hounds.

never been fortified. The palace was grouped around a central courtyard and the ground-floor rooms were mainly used for storage and for workshops, while the remains of great staircases showed that the state apartments must have been at first-floor level. In the west wing was a ceremonial throne room with its throne still in position. The walls had been covered with colorful frescoes. Also in the west wing was a series of long narrow cellars with huge storage jars, as high as a man, for grain, or wine, or oil. Remains of hundreds of these jars were found in lines along the walls of the cellars. In the floors were stone-lined tanks, also for storage. In this area, Evans soon began to discover many inscribed clay tablets with some form of ancient writing on them.

Within a few weeks he had found hundreds. He had also found the clay impressions of seals. The engraved seals had been stamped onto the clay when it was still wet, securing the strings that had tied bundles or boxes of clay tablets. The language was unknown, but Evans soon saw that some of the signs roughly represented creatures or objects – man, pig, chariot, and so on. He suggested, and time was to prove him correct, that the tablets represented a system of recording goods or creatures that were being received into the palace or traded for other goods. One group of tablets seemed especially to refer to weapons, such as swords, arrowheads, and chariots.

Evans also uncovered the remains of frescoes. In an entrance corridor, he found part of a processional scene, and by the northern approach he uncovered a splendid charging bull. A further fresco showed young men and girls making acrobatic leaps over the horns of a charging bull. With the discovery of these bull pictures, an ancient Greek story suddenly came alive. This was the legend of the Minotaur, a huge bull-like monster kept in a labyrinth at Knossos. It fed each year on seven youths and seven maidens sent by the Athenians. The story relates that Theseus, the great hero of the Greeks, was sent one year to be one of the Minotaur's victims. Ariadne, the daughter of King Minos of Crete, fell in love with Theseus. She gave him a sword to kill the monster and a thread to unwind as he entered the labyrinth and later follow to find his way out.

It is easy to see how that vast, complicated palace, with its endless corridors, stairways, and maze of rooms, could come to be thought of as a labyrinth. It has also been proved that the great Minoan civilization (named after Minos, the king of Crete) was at its most powerful between 1650 and 1540 B.C. In those days it was greater than the settlements on the mainland of Greece, such as Mycenae and Athens. Those cities must have undoubtedly sent tribute and goods to the Minoans, though not young people for sacrifice.

About 1450 B.C., a disaster must have befallen the Minoans. For some unknown reason, Knossos was destroyed. The Minoans, a great seafaring nation, had built up their kingdom on trade. Their ships sailed as far as the Nile in Egypt with oil and wine, and their pottery and metal objects have been found all over the Mediterranean. They must have greatly influenced the people of mainland Greece, for the Mycenaeans

Fresco found at Knossos showing acrobats vaulting over a charging bull.

seem to have developed their civilization after a similar pattern. Excavations carried out at Mycenae in 1952 revealed that outside the city walls had stood many houses which must have belonged to merchants. In these houses were found large storage jars of the Minoan type, great numbers of ivory carvings, and clay tablets inscribed with writing similar to that which Evans found on the clay tablets at Knossos. It was clear that the Mycenaeans, like the Minoans, relied for their wealth on trade with far-off lands and that they enjoyed many of the activities that had delighted the Minoans. Schliemann himself had found at Tiryns a fresco of a man balancing on a bull's back.

One important discovery remains to be mentioned: the deciphering of the writing on the many clay tablets that had been found at Knossos, Mycenae, Pylos, and other places in the Mediter-

ranean. It was in 1890, the year before Schliemann's death, that an archaeologist working in a tomb chamber at Mycenae first found an example of Mycenaean writing on the handles of two vessels. But it was not until 1952 that an Englishman, Michael Ventris, demonstrated what language this was. He had assembled all the signs that had been found on the many clay tablets and worked out how they related to one another. He then tried to substitute for an often repeated syllable what seemed to be a likely sound. Suddenly all the pieces fell into place and he found himself reading a language like ancient Greek. The Greek language was proved to be one of the oldest in existence. Words spoken at Knossos in 1500 B.C. can still be heard in Athens today.

II The story of Agamemnon

Palace life at Mycenae

In his early childhood, Agamemnon spent most of his time with his mother and the ladies who kept her company. Men rarely came into the women's quarters in the palace of Mycenae. The women had their own hall in which they spent most of the day weaving, spinning, or making beautiful flowing dresses which fell in folds from their shoulders. As a baby, Agamemnon was fascinated by the golden brooches, necklaces and earrings worn by his mother, the queen of Mycenae. As she moved in the sunlight which filtered down through the high windows of the hall, the gold flashed warmly against the pure white of her robes. Sometimes she would take him out into the palace garden. All around them were the white stone walls of the palace, and from its many rooms and from the city beyond came the sounds of voices and much activity, contrasting with the peaceful garden with its olive trees and vine-covered pathways.

One of his earliest memories was of a story that his mother used to tell him, of the ancient hero Jason. Jason and his brave companions sailed across the sea to Colchis to find a golden fleece guarded by a dragon. With the help of Eros, the god of love, Jason managed to steal the fleece. This story was typical of many of the tales Agamemnon heard of the heroes of the past. It made him realize that when he grew to manhood he too must be a hero, strong, brave, and clever, and that he must keep the gods on his side and please them by offering them sacrifices. But, for the time being, he must stay with the women and the other children. He spent some of his time playing games, often with a ball or checkers. In one favorite game, all the boys split up into pairs and one from each pair climbed on the back of his partner, sitting on his shoulders as if he were riding a horse.

Occasionally, he would go to watch the women making cloth. First of all they would clean and dye the wool that had been sheared from the sheep. When it was dry, Agamemnon would help tease the wool to make it fluffy, and then comb it, ready for the spinners to twist into yarn. His mother had a silver basket on wheels which was filled with yarn of all colors. She would take her threads from this basket when she was standing at her weaving frame. Agamemnon would watch,

fascinated, as his mother skillfully passed the shuttle that drew the colored threads back and forth across the weaving loom.

Soon the carefree days of childhood passed; one day the Queen took him through the palace into a room he had not visited before. It was his father's room, and it led off the megaron, or men's hall. Agamemnon was amazed by it, for the walls were covered with colorful paintings of people in processions and of scenes in which men hunted wild boar with a pack of hounds. The heavy metal door to the megaron swung open, and at once Agamemnon could hear the sound of men's voices, talking and laughing. His father Atreus, the King of Mycenae, stood before him. Agamemnon was a little frightened: he had seen his father on only a few occasions before this day, and had never been alone with him before. But his father smiled, sat down on one of the fine, polished wooden chairs inlaid with ivory, and beckoned Agamemnon to sit at his feet. The young prince was quick to obey.

That afternoon, Agamemnon learned about his future. Atreus told him that one day he would become King of Mycenae, with all the city and the countryside around it under his command. Now he must leave the women and play his part in the life of the megaron. He would be taught to read, to understand the trading customs of Mycenae and to play his part in the sacrifices to the gods. Above all, he would be trained to use arms and to fight, for a king could only survive if he were a great warrior.

From this point on, Agamemnon's life was full of activity and each day had a regular pattern. He spent a couple of hours exercising his body under the direction of his trainers, learning how to use all his muscles to the greatest advantage in running or jumping, and how to cast large stones great distances. Other young noblemen in the palace trained with him every day and competed against him in sprinting and jumping. Sometimes they went out of the city, through the Lion Gate, along the road lined with the houses and storerooms of wealthy merchants. This brought them into the countryside, where vines and olive trees grew in abundance. Here the farmers made wine and olive oil and fattened their sheep, bullocks, and goats. On these outings the young men would run for a mile then walk for a mile until they reached the river. There, while they rested beneath the olive and cypress trees, their slaves would prepare a meal on the river's bank. After swimming, they would rub their bodies all over with olive oil, get dressed, and return refreshed and cheerful in horse-drawn carts to Mycenae.

Education of a prince

Not all of Agamemnon's boyhood days were spent in such pleasant ways as exercising, playing sports, and swimming with his fellows. Every day he spent some hours with his tutors, for there was much to learn. To begin with, he had to learn to read and to write. The tutor would come to the lesson carrying a pot containing wet clay and a small wooden board which had raised edges, making a sort of frame. The tutor would take a handful of clay and spread it over the board. He then ran a piece of wood over the clay so that it filled the frame and the surface was smooth and level with the frame's raised edges. Then he would take a pointed stick and Agamemnon would watch fascinated as he made marks, lines, and little pictures in the still wet clay. He soon learned what the signs meant. The simpler signs represented sounds, just as our letters stand for the different speaking sounds that make up our language, but the little pictures were different; they stood for objects, or animals, or for a man, or a woman. It was important that Agamemnon learn how to read because the people of Mycenae kept all their records of trading with the other nations around the Mediterranean in this way.

Among the products traded was obsidian, the valuable and useful natural glass from the Lipari

ᛉ ͨ	MAN
▢	CLOTH
帚	WINE

Islands that was used to make knife blades and other tools. The tin and silver that came from Etruria and southern Iberia were also traded, together with the iron from the land of the Chalybes that was used to make weapons and armor. The tutor took Agamemnon to see the farmers treading grapes to make wine, and taught him about the working life of the city of Mycenae. They visited the furniture makers, potters, and goldsmiths. The goldsmiths would hammer their gold to an amazing thinness before fashioning it into a useful or decorative article.

As he grew older, Agamemnon played a more and more important part in the worship of the gods. He was taught how to hold the sacred vessel while it was filled with the consecrated wine from the shrine, and to carry it in procession to his father in the megaron. As the procession entered the megaron his father would stand up to receive the vessel from him. Then, in silence, Atreus the king would move to the hearth in the center of the hall, around which stood four great pillars. He would pour the wine into the shallow trough that surrounded the fire. This was the libation to the gods, and, as the wine steamed and hissed before the great log fire, the bard would sing praises to the mother goddess of the earth, and to the other gods who defended Mycenae from her enemies and provided for her needs.

Agamemnon also learned to serve at the shrine of the palace of Mycenae. This was a small room, containing beautiful statues and ritual vessels, which was used only by members of the royal family. (Each household in the city had its own shrine, though humbler and less grandly equipped than the king's, for the Mycenaeans did not build temples in which many people could worship together.) Agamemnon had to stand in the shrine holding the sacrificial victim – a dove, or a lamb, or some other small animal – and place it between the horns of consecration, shaped like the horns on a bull's head. This showed the god that he was offering the creature to him. Then he would take the victim to a stone altar which stood on three legs in the center of the small room, and, looking up at the small clay statues of the gods and goddesses which stood on a raised platform at the end of the shrine, he would plunge the sacrificial knife into the animal and let its blood flow on to the altar.

As Agamemnon became a young man, his skill in all the arts of warfare and sport increased. The wrestling games of his childhood became more serious and he learned all that a young warrior had to know about man-to-man combat. He became skilled in moving swiftly before his opponent with his short sword in one hand and his dagger in the other, so that his foe would not know when or where he was going to strike. He was trained to throw the javelin with force and accuracy and learned how to string a bow and shoot arrows. From his boyhood he had practiced horsemanship; and now, as a young man, he became skillful at driving chariots. The light two-wheeled vehicles were drawn by two powerful horses, and the charioteer had to know how to guide them and whip them just enough to encourage them to go like the wind. Soon Agamemnon was a fine charioteer, outstripping even the older warriors with years of experience. He was only seventeen when he first won a chariot race. These were held down on the plain below Mycenae, as part of the sports held to greet the rebirth of the year each springtime. In the years that followed he never failed to win, for he always managed to keep perfect balance in the swaying, speeding chariot.

The great hall

The evening of the day when Agamemnon first won the chariot race was one that he would never forget. He drove in triumph back up into the city, through the Lion Gate and on into the central courtyard before the megaron. Atreus, his father, stood beside him in the swaying chariot, and the townspeople followed them cheering. The horses were unyoked and the chariot left propped up against a wall in the courtyard near the sacrificial slab. The men went to wash and rub their bodies down with fresh and sweet-smelling olive oil and to put on clean robes in preparation for the great feast later in the evening. At the appointed hour, they all gathered together in the courtyard. There, on the sacrificial altar which stood immediately opposite the pillared entrance to the megaron, twelve sheep, eight boars, and two oxen were killed with great ceremony. Offerings were made to the gods, and then portions of the flesh were brought into the hall and roasted on spits in front of the great fire of cedar and sandalwood. Here were also cooked black puddings, made by putting blood and fat into the paunch of an animal. The king sat on his stone seat on the side of the hall facing the hearth. Around him, sitting and lying on beds and seats with sheepskin covers, were assembled all the nobles and high-ranking citi-

zens of Mycenae. Long tables were at once set before them. The slaves circulated among the gathering, bringing platters of roasted meat, meal cakes, and puddings, and filling the golden and silver wine cups from great golden flagons of wine. As the wine warmed the hearts of the company, the laughter, shouting and joyfulness increased.

Darkness began to fall and, at a signal given by Atreus, three braziers were set up in the hall to give light. They were piled up with faggots of wood, long seasoned and dry. Mid-way between the braziers stood young girls, taking turns to hold up flaming torches. The firelight cast a glow on the happy faces and shone from the armor hung on the walls and the sheaves of gleaming spears standing around the central pillars. When the company had eaten its fill of meat, meal cakes, fruit, and other delicacies, there was a pause. Next, an old, blind man was led by the hand out into the center of the hall. As he sat down, a small harp was handed to him, and he began to strum his harp and sing tales of heroes, both ancient and recent, while all the people, suddenly silent, listened intently. Later there was dancing in which Agamemnon and the other young men took part. At long last, when they were all too tired to feast or dance any longer, Atreus and his family rose and went to their beds, while the others lay down in the megaron and slept.

Death of a king

Agamemnon was nearly thirty and married when the king, Atreus, fell ill. It was soon clear that he was dying. Despite this sorrow and worry, Agamemnon could not afford to waste any time in gaining the support of all the important men in Mycenae. He promised them great gifts of gold and other valuables if they agreed to hail him as the new king on Atreus' death.

Preparations were also made for the burial of Atreus and for the great feast and funeral games to follow his death. Earlier in his reign, Atreus had built the grandest of all tombs in the hillside below the city, outside the walls. It was made from skillfully curved blocks of stone fitted together to form a circular vaulted dome. The chamber inside was 49.5 feet (15 meters) across, and the highest point of the dome, where the curving sides met, was 42.9 feet (13 meters) above the ground. This vast dome was covered with bands of bronze and hundreds of golden rosettes. Its great doorway was surrounded by carvings and fitted with doors 18.2 feet (5.5 meters) high. A passageway, 115.5 feet (35 meters) long, was cut through the hillside to the tomb and lined with stone walls.

The day after Atreus' death, his body was taken into the megaron. There, watched by Agamemnon, his weeping mother, and other

close relatives and friends, the dead king was dressed in his robes of state. His golden diadem was placed on his head, his seals of office were attached to his wrist, and his favorite dagger was placed by his side. His body was then carried out on a bier to a chariot drawn by the two finest horses in the royal stables. A long, solemn procession formed behind the chariot as it moved slowly through the city, out of the Lion Gate and down through the lower city to the tomb entrance. Crowds lined the route. The chariot turned up the long passageway to the tomb's doorway. Agamemnon and the other mourners followed.

At the great doorway, the vast, heavy bronze doors swung back. In the cool darkness of the tomb, the bronze and gold of the vault gleamed magically. Atreus was laid down inside on a carpet of beaten gold. Around him were placed fine golden and pottery vessels full of the food, wine, oil, and ointments he would need on his last journey. Weapons of war lay nearby: swords, rapiers, daggers, and spears, a mighty shield to cover the whole body, a quiver full of arrows, and a bow. He would need these to defend himself against any evil spirits which might try to bar his way into the other world. To the sound of a solemn incantation, Agamemnon took up a thin-bladed sword and bent the blade to release the spirit of the sword for the service of its master. Next, the horses waiting outside in the passageway were killed, and their bodies brought into the tomb where they were carefully laid out to face each other in death. Rams and other sacrificial animals were slaughtered too. Fires were lit, and when the sacrifices had been roasted, all the mourners in the tomb sat down to share the funeral banquet. Many had little stomach for food, but it was necessary to share this last meal with the dead man. While the embers of the fire still glowed, Agamemnon and his friends carefully laid in place their last presents for Atreus before leaving the tomb, taking care as they did so not to tread on any of the precious objects, weapons, food, or slaughtered horses covering the floor. Outside in the entrance passage, blinking from the sudden glare of the sun, the mourners watched the bronze doors close. Slaves then filled in the passageway with earth. A day later, the tomb of Atreus would be entirely covered by a simple mound of earth. Agamemnon was king.

For the rest of that day and the two days following, all the people of Mycenae attended the funeral games held in honor of the dead king. Agamemnon did not take part in these games, but presided over them and gave out the prizes. Now that he was king, he was set apart from other men.

Agamemnon's domain

As soon as Agamemnon became King of Mycenae, his days were almost completely occupied with the duties of his office. As king, he owned the largest share of land in his kingdom. Some of this land was held by other men, who owed him service and taxes in return. Agamemnon's private estate was situated near an important religious center close to Mycenae. Next to the king, the most important man in Mycenae was the leader of the war host. He was responsible for gathering a great army of soldiers together should they at any time be needed. Quite frequently, Agamemnon had to spend time with him discussing the numbers of men, weapons, and other equipment that could at any time be brought from different parts of the kingdom. When not with the leader of the war host, Agamemnon was often with his companions, who were all nobles with large estates. As such, they could provide him with military support. They were among the men who gathered in the megaron for the great occasions of feasting. The remaining land in the kingdom was owned by the gods and goddesses and by organizations of the common people. The priests of the gods and goddesses received offerings of many kinds – gold, grain, oil, wine, and honey – and they employed large numbers of people, including slaves. The common people shared their land so that each family had enough to live on. The king was chief over all this complicated organization. He received taxes of oil, grain, and animals, and in return he protected the kingdom against foreign rulers. Throughout the year, visitors could be seen trailing up the road to Mycenae with their carts or animals laden with taxes. They would be received by the tax collector in his office. Tax records were kept on clay tablets.

As well as concerning himself with the running of his own kingdom, Agamemnon maintained contact with the other chiefs of the separate kingdoms within Greece, such as Pylos, Sparta, and Tiryns, his nearest neighbor. Since Mycenae was the wealthiest and most powerful of these kingdoms, Agamemnon was overlord of Greece and able to call on the support of the other kings in time of war.

Mycenae's wealth was the result of a flourishing foreign trade with places as far apart as Britain in the west and Egypt in the east. Long ago, the empire of the Minoans, which was centered at Knossos in Crete, had been conquered by the Mycenaeans, and they had been quick to use the trading routes set up by the Minoans. As well as the obsidian from the Lipari Islands, the tin and silver from Etruria and Iberia, ivory was brought from Syria, and amber beads from Britain. The most valuable and important of the metals, gold, came from Egypt. Agamemnon, like the kings of Mycenae before him, was careful to maintain

good relations with the Egyptian pharaoh. Since the Mycenaeans were such good fighters, the pharaoh often called on Agamemnon for supplies of well-trained soldiers in return for gold.

Below the city walls of Mycenae was the lower town where wealthy merchants lived and controlled the export of sweet-smelling oil, wool, and woolen cloth from Mycenaean ports. Agamemnon himself owned a large building in this area and took much interest in encouraging the making of perfumes and cloth that went on in the house. He also continued the work of beautifying the palace of Mycenae, and like his father and grandfather before him he encouraged skilled craftsmen from Crete and other places to come and carry on their trades in Mycenae. In the lower city were makers of furniture, who fashioned tables and stools from ebony and inlaid the wood with beautifully carved pieces of ivory, gold, and other metals. There were potters, too, who made delicate cups and other vessels and painted them with hunting or battle scenes. There were also goldsmiths, who fashioned the metal into ornaments for clothes and vessels for use by the royal household of Mycenae.

In the first few years of his reign, Agamemnon made sure that the busy trading and manufacturing life of Mycenae continued to flourish. It was well he did so, for events abroad were soon to force him to leave Mycenae for a long period.

The call to arms

For generations Mycenae had enjoyed a flourishing trade with the Mediterranean and beyond, and had grown rich and powerful. In recent years, however, merchants and traders had begun to complain because their ships were being interfered with by the Trojans. Troy, a prosperous and powerful city, commanded an important trade route with the east, for it was situated at the entrance to the Black Sea. The Trojans kept vast flocks of sheep and were the great rivals of the Mycenaeans in the wool and cloth trade. The rivalry was the cause of some ill feeling between the two cities. In the early part of Agamemnon's reign, matters grew worse, for reports reached him that Greek ships returning from the Black Sea area, laden with cargoes of corn, were being held by the Trojans. The Mycenaeans depended on corn from the lands around the Black Sea to feed their ever-growing population. Agamemnon and his counselors debated the problem and sent protests to Troy, but there was little they could do without waging a full-scale war. This they were reluctant to do, for Troy lay far off across the sea; the journey would be long and dangerous, and the outcome of such a war uncertain.

An unexpected crisis arose. One day, a servant came to report that chariots and horsemen could be seen approaching Mycenae in great haste. The visitor was none other than Menelaus, King of Sparta and Agamemnon's brother. He was both agitated and angry. Recently Paris, a son of Priam, the King of Troy, had visited Sparta, and the hospitable Menelaus had made him very welcome; but Paris had repaid him by stealing away his wife, Helen, one of the world's most beautiful women. The pair were now on their way back to Troy. Agamemnon was horrified: all the indignation that he had suffered from the Trojans over matters of trade rose up in him at this insult. Menelaus urged him to make war on Troy without delay, but Agamemnon first sent a message by swift ship to Troy demanding Helen's instant return. Priam sent back an insolent reply asking Agamemnon why he was making so much fuss over one woman, and reminding him of all the women of Asia that the Greeks had stolen.

This reply was what finally made Agamemnon declare war, for the theft of Helen was a crime committed by a guest against his host – an unforgivable sin in Greek eyes. So he sent messengers to all the kings and princes of Greece, asking them to gather together men and arms, to have ships built, and to meet at the port of Aulis on the coast near Thebes, the Boeotian capital.

The whole of Mycenae was now caught up in preparations for the war. Craftsmen set to work hammering out bronze and iron for more swords, daggers, spears, armor, and shields. New chariots that were easy to dismantle and powerful bows for use with iron-tipped arrows were also made.

At Nauplia, on the coast south of Mycenae, many ships were being constructed on slipways, each with a single mast and a square sail.

All the heroes of Greece had gladly answered Agamemnon's appeal for military support: all but Odysseus of Ithaca, who was said to have gone mad.

Agamemnon and Menelaus were anxious to investigate this strange rumor. Accompanied by Palamedes, the prince of Nauplia, they went to the isle of Ithaca, where they found Odysseus plowing the sand on the seashore; an ox and a horse were harnessed to his plow and he was sowing not seeds but salt. It seemed he *was* mad. Palamedes, however, was suspicious. To test Odysseus, he put Telemachus, the baby son of Odysseus and his wife Penelope, in front of the plow. When Odysseus saw his beloved son in danger, he stopped the plow at once: his pretended madness was over. He explained that he had not wanted to leave his wife and child and the island home that he loved, and had pretended to be mad because an oracle had warned him that if he went to Troy he would not return home for twenty years. Nevertheless, he agreed to ignore the warning.

War and sacrifice

The great fleet set sail, with Agamemnon in command of the whole army, and Odysseus, Diomedes, and Palamedes as seconds-in-command. Nestor, the wise old king of Pylos, was Agamemnon's chief adviser, and Achilles was admiral of the fleet. But Achilles did not prove a very good admiral. He led the fleet so badly that it landed at Mysia, several hundred miles to the south of Troy, where, thinking that they had actually reached Trojan lands, the Greeks set about ravaging the countryside and burning down the villages. When they realized their mistake, they set sail again, but a terrible storm came up which scattered the ships far and wide and drove most of them back toward Greece.

Agamemnon and a large portion of the fleet came to land in his own country of Argolis, so he returned to Mycenae while the ships were being repaired. He told the other kings and princes of Greece to assemble once more at Aulis the following spring. There they waited for a favorable wind to take them toward Troy, but a dead calm lay over the sea day after day and they were unable to set sail. At last, a prophet called Calchas told Agamemnon that he would never be able to sail to Troy until he sacrificed his daughter Iphigenia to the goddess Artemis. Agamemnon was filled with sorrow, but, telling himself that Greece must come before any personal matter, he gave orders for the sacrifice. Iphigenia displayed great courage and was hailed by the army as a great heroine in the struggle against Troy. But the goddess Artemis took pity on her and, just as the knife was falling, she snatched her away and left in her place a young deer.

After Iphigenia's bravery, the wind rose strongly from the west, and the great fleet set out once again for Troy. They went ashore on the island of Tenedos, a few miles from the Trojan coast, while Menelaus and Odysseus went ahead as ambassadors. The two heroes marched inland across the Trojan plain to the city itself, where they were received coldly by all except Antenor, a cousin of King Priam, who offered them the hospitality of his house. On the following day, the two Greeks attended an assembly of Trojan lords and princes. They made three requests: for Helen to be restored, suitable fines to be paid, and hostages provided. The Trojans were impressed by the words and bearing of Odysseus and Menelaus, and many felt that they should agree to the requests. But Paris had bribed some members of the assembly to urge that Helen must be kept and the two ambassadors murdered. They would indeed have been murdered if Antenor had not smuggled them swiftly out of the city.

When the ambassadors had returned and told their story to the fleet, the Greeks were filled with rage and indignation at the treachery of the Trojans. The Greeks decided to land at once and take their revenge. As the fleet sailed in close to the beach, the Trojan army came rushing down to try to stop the Greeks' landing. The Greeks poured out of their ships and immediately began to fight. A terrible battle was fought that day. Many great deeds were done, but both sides lost many fine warriors.

For a long time that day, the Greeks were held back by a Trojan hero called Cycnus. He was the son of the god Poseidon and could not be killed by any weapon. He slaughtered large numbers of the Greek army. Achilles rushed to do battle with him but found that neither his spear nor his sword could pierce Cycnus. Achilles was enraged and, thrusting his shield in Cycnus' face, he forced him to step back and at the same time skillfully tripped him up. Achilles jumped on the fallen Cycnus and, mustering all his strength, strangled him with the straps of his own helmet.

As soon as the Trojans realized that Cycnus was slain, a great cry went up. They fled back into the city of Troy, barred the gates and stationed soldiers around all the walls and towers of the city to hold back the Greeks, refusing to venture out again. So the Greeks advanced across the Trojan plain, set up a formidable encampment around the city, and laid siege to it. They tried to stop all food and reinforcements from being taken into the city in order to starve the Trojans into despair and defeat. But Troy was very large, and the Trojans were powerful both within the city and in the surrounding countryside. Try as they might, the Greeks could never completely blockade Troy. The Trojans never suffered the full hardships of a long siege. They had plenty of water and could always obtain food. Also, from time to time, reinforcements were able to win their way through the Greek encampment into the city.

So the Greeks failed to take Troy in a single surprise attack, and so the ten-year-long siege began. Gradually, as time passed, the Greeks overran the countryside around the city and sacked other towns under Trojan rule or in league with Troy. Many a city was besieged, attacked, and destroyed, and had all its valuables taken by Agamemnon's men. Greek ships went back and forth across the sea, taking loot and slaves to Greece and bringing food, supplies, and reinforcements back to the warriors.

Attack on Troy

As the years passed and the Greeks were no nearer to conquering Troy and returning home, they became increasingly restless and irritable with one another. Disagreements broke out among their leaders. One quarrel, between Agamemnon and Achilles, the greatest fighter in the Greek army, became so bitter that Achilles refused to play any further part in the fighting. He retired, sulking, to his tent and hung up his armor. So did Patroclus, his cousin, and all the host of the Myrmidons under their command. Achilles swore to fight only if his ships were in danger.

When news of the quarrel between Agamemnon and Achilles reached Troy, the Trojans themselves decided to march out and scatter the Greeks while their greatest fighter was sulking in his tent. So the two armies met on the level plains before Troy. The Trojan and Mycenaean armies used a special formation for such battles. First they drew up their charioteers in a long line to head the charge. Behind them, they formed a square out of the foot soldiers, with the sturdy, reliable fighters on the outside of the square and the cowards in the middle. Often, a battle would become a series of combats between champions, with the others cheering on the hero from their own side. This is what happened that day.

Suddenly Paris, the Trojan who had abducted Menelaus' wife Helen, was seized with unexpected boldness and offered to meet Menelaus in single combat: if he killed Menelaus, the Greeks must swear to return home without Helen; but if Menelaus should kill *him*, Helen would be returned to Greece with great treasure. Since the Greeks were so tired of the long war, they agreed to this proposal. Both sides swore to keep the truce and to let the fight between

Menelaus and Paris determine the war's outcome.

A sacrifice was made to the gods, and then Paris and Menelaus stepped forward from the ranks of their armies, formed in long lines to watch the fight while sitting on the ground. The two warriors wore *greaves*, pieces of armor shaped to cover the legs up to the knees and fastened at the ankles with silver clasps; on their chests, they wore well-fitting corselets of beaten bronze. Across the shoulders of each man hung a strap carrying a fine sword of bronze with silver studs. Each carried a shield of bull's hide and a strong ash-wood spear with a bronze point. Their helmets, with side pieces to protect the cheeks and neck, were topped by tall crests of horsehair.

First Paris hurled his spear, which was stopped by the shield of Menelaus. The point was turned and it did not pierce the shield. Then Menelaus threw his spear. Driven by the might born of his anger, the spear passed through Paris' shield and pierced his bronze breastplate. But the blade merely grazed his side. With a great cry, Menelaus leaped forward and, seizing Paris by the crest of his helmet, began to drag him toward the Greek forces. Paris would have been strangled by the straps of his own helmet had they not suddenly snapped. His valor left him and he fled back to Troy.

Menelaus proclaimed himself the winner, since his adversary had, in his cowardice, fled from the fight, and all men believed that the war was over. So it would have been, had not the Trojan Pandarus acted treacherously. For, when he saw Menelaus in triumph, he let fly an arrow that wounded Menelaus in the side. The Greeks, outraged at his breach of the truce, immediately began to arm. The Trojans did so too, and so began the fiercest battle of the war.

At first the Trojans gave ground and were driven back toward Troy. But Hector, the Trojan's champion warrior, came down from the city and rallied his forces so effectively that the Greeks were driven back to the very seashore. Some of their ships were set on fire. In desperation Patroclus went to his cousin and begged the mighty Achilles to let him lead the Myrmidons into battle, since Achilles would not do so himself. Reluctantly, Achilles agreed, and Patroclus went into the fight wearing Achilles' armor.

Hector thought that Achilles himself had entered the battle, and so challenged him to individual combat. But Patroclus' strength was no match for that of Hector. The combat ended with Patroclus, dressed in Achilles' armor, being killed by Hector. Achilles, wild with grief at the death of his cousin, made peace with Agamemnon and began once again to play an active part in the conflict. After the funeral rites for Patroclus, Achilles issued a challenge to Hector. In the fierce combat that followed, Hector was killed.

Although this event did not conclude the Trojan war, the death of Hector was a terrible blow to the morale of the city. Hector had been the finest leader as well as the greatest fighter among the Trojans. The clouds of doom were gathering above Troy.

Helen recognized him in spite of his disguise. She won Odysseus' confidence by telling him how desperately she wished to return to Sparta and to her husband Menelaus, and how she had frequently tried to escape from Troy. The pair made plans for the Palladium to be stolen.

Once the Palladium had been smuggled out of Troy, Odysseus planned the final overthrow of the city. He ordered a great number of trees to be felled on the nearby Mount Ida and the timber to be carried back to the Greek camp. There a high wall had been built to hide the activities of the Greek army from the Trojans. The timber was cut and shaped and made into a vast wooden horse. It was ornamented with jewels and gold, and in its belly was a great hollow, large enough for thirty men to lie concealed with all their armor and weapons. Under the belly of the horse was a secret trapdoor, so skillfully made that no one could see it from the outside. The horse stood on wheels and was so high and wide that it could not pass through any of the gates of Troy.

As soon as the horse was finished, Agamemnon ordered the walls around the camp to be destroyed, the camp to be leveled, and the whole army to put to sea. The Greeks left behind only

The defeat of Troy

Troy fell at last through the skill and cunning of Odysseus, King of Ithaca, who had pretended madness to avoid going to war against Troy.

It happened in a strange way. After Hector's death, the Trojans, under the command of Paris, took the field for the last time. In this battle Philoctetes, a Greek, mortally wounded Paris with a poisoned arrow. With Paris dead, Helen was free, but even now the Trojans had no intention of sending her back to Menelaus. Instead, Deiphobus and Helenus, two of Paris' brothers, quarreled as to which of them should marry her. When their father, Priam, gave Helen to Deiphobus, Helenus left Troy to join the Greeks.

By this time, Agamemnon and his companions were at their wits' end to know why Troy had not yet fallen. Helenus was able to tell them the reason: there was in the city a sacred and magical stone, called the Palladium, which had been cast down from heaven by Zeus, the king of the gods. No city in which the Palladium rested could fall.

When he heard this, the resourceful Odysseus disguised himself as a beggar and managed to gain entrance to Troy by pretending that he had been beaten and driven away by the Greeks.

thirty of their finest warriors, hidden in the belly of the horse. When the next day dawned, the Trojans looked out from their city walls and saw only the monstrous horse towered there.

At first, the Trojans were undecided as to what should be done with the horse. They could see letters of gold on its side which read, "For their return home, the Greeks dedicate this thanks-offering to Athena," and so many believed that it must be taken into Troy and placed in the temple of Athena. Others were suspicious and thought it was a trick. But Odysseus had instructed his cousin Sinon how to deceive the Trojans. Sinon told them that he would have been sacrificed to the horse had he not escaped. He explained that the Greeks had made the beast so large in order to stop the Trojans from taking it into their city, for it would make the city impossible to conquer.

The Trojans rejoiced at the ending of the war and at their good fortune. They garlanded the horse with flowers, tore down a section of the city wall, and towed it into the courtyard before the temple of Athena. That night all the people of Troy feasted and drank in celebration of the Greeks' departure. Soon not one sober Trojan

remained, and few guards or sentries were posted.

Meanwhile, the Greek fleet stole back to the beaches in the silence of the night before the moon rose, and Helen placed a bright light in her window to guide the Greeks back to Troy. Odysseus and his men sat silently in the belly of the horse until, as the first beams of the moon shone, Odysseus gave the signal. They climbed down out of the horse, crept through the silent streets, killed what few sentries were on guard, and opened all the gates of Troy to Agamemnon and his army.

That was a night of terrible slaughter. Death fell on the Trojans before they were awake and able to arm. The frustration of the ten-year siege had built up such fury in the Greeks that they were merciless in bringing about the total destruction of the city. Yet there were some acts of kindness. Odysseus, remembering the courtesy that had been shown him by Antenor, helped him and his wife to escape from the burning city. King Agamemnon saw the pious Aeneas, a Trojan prince, walking through the streets with his old father Anchises on his shoulders, and leading by the hand his little son Ascanius, while Creusa his wife followed behind. He was so touched at this picture of family unity that he gave orders that they were to be spared. But few survived the Greek attack and Troy was never again a powerful city.

Agamemnon's return

The fall of Troy was not the end of adventure and bloodshed for the Greek heroes. Agamemnon's fate was particularly tragic. While he had been away from Mycenae, his wife Clytemnestra had come to hate him more and more. She was bitter about the way he had sought to sacrifice their daughter Iphigenia at Aulis when the fleet was waiting to depart for Troy, and she hated being left alone in Mycenae for so long. So she took a lover, Aegisthus, and married him.

News of the fall of Troy was brought to Mycenae by a series of bonfires which were lit on the tops of high mountains. Clytemnestra kept a watchman constantly posted to look for the signal, for she had not told Agamemnon about Aegisthus. When news came of the ending of the war, she sent Orestes, her son, away to stay with his uncle, and she concealed her two daughters, Electra and Chrysothemis, in the palace. The cowardly Aegisthus hid himself away while the treacherous queen went out to greet Agamemnon.

Agamemnon sped across the plain towards Mycenae in great excitement and joy. This was the moment to which he had looked forward for ten years, the moment when, as conquering hero, he returned home in glory, bringing many captured slaves and much treasure. Clytemnestra made him welcome and increased his joy by leading him through the cheering crowds to the palace. Then she took him to the marble-floored bathroom and told the slave women to leave, for she would bathe and anoint him with her own hands. She brought him wine to drink and delicacies to eat. As she soothed his body with her hands, Agamemnon felt, for the first time in years,

Eventually, Aegisthus grew angry with Electra, for she constantly threatened and taunted him, and he decided to have her taken away and imprisoned. In great haste, she sent word to Orestes. Now he knew that the moment for action had come. He arrived at Mycenae in disguise and went to Electra, who was overjoyed to see him. They worked out a plan. Orestes, in disguise, would go to Aegisthus and tell him that all danger was past because Orestes had died. Then Aegisthus would be off his guard. Meanwhile, Electra would send word to her mother that she was ill and wanted Clytemnestra near her.

The plot worked perfectly. Aegisthus was so pleased with the news that he invited the disguised – and unrecognized – Orestes to join him in a sacrifice to the gods. At the sacrifice, Orestes killed Aegisthus and told the people of Mycenae who he was. At once they hailed him as their king, for they were glad to have the son of Agamemnon as their ruler and to be rid of the tyrannous Aegisthus. But Orestes had to complete his act of vengeance, and, when he slew his mother also, the Mycenaeans were deeply shocked. They prepared to stone him to death.

At this moment, the god Apollo appeared and told the people that they must not harm Orestes, for he had done the deed by divine command. He told them that Orestes must wander for a year in exile, and, at the end of that time, he would return to be their king. This is what happened. Orestes had many adventures in his year of penance. At the end of it, he married Hermione, the granddaughter of the old king of Sparta, returned to Mycenae with his bride, and reigned happily.

complete peace of mind. After he had bathed, his wife handed him a finely embroidered shirt to wear and urged him to hurry and make ready for the feast which awaited them. She slipped the garment over his head. While he struggled inside it (his wife had sewn up the sleeves and neck) she struck him with an axe. Then the cowardly Aegisthus came out of his hiding place and helped to kill the noble and brave Agamemnon. So it was that this fearless warrior, who had led the forces of Greece for ten years against Troy, was treacherously killed by his wife and her lover.

Clytemnestra and Aegisthus ruled in Mycenae after Agamemnon's burial. But Aegisthus felt anxious that Orestes, Agamemnon's son, might return to take revenge for his father's death, and he tried to find out where Orestes was living in order to murder him. But Clytemnestra was not quite so evil as to slay her own son, and so she kept his whereabouts hidden. In the meantime, she caused her daughter Electra to be married to a poor peasant near Mycenae so that she might not have a powerful husband who could punish Clytemnestra and Aegisthus. For the next seven years, matters remained thus, but Electra kept in touch with Orestes while he grew up at his uncle's court. She often sent messages to remind him that he must one day avenge his father's death.

The wanderings of Odysseus

Odysseus, the cleverest of the Greek princes, whose brilliant wooden horse plan had finally led to the fall of Troy, had meanwhile experienced enough adventures for several lifetimes.

In the land of the Cyclopes in Sicily, Odysseus and twelve of his men came across a giant's cave. The giant, whose name was Polyphemus, was a Cyclops, a fearsome creature of enormous size with a single eye in the middle of his forehead. When the giant returned with his flock of sheep he found Odysseus and his men. Odysseus tried to explain who they all were, but, despite their appeals, Polyphemus immediately grabbed two of the men, dashed out their brains on the floor, and ate them for his supper, bones and all. The following morning, he ate two more of the men and went out, having imprisoned the rest in the cave by rolling an enormous stone across the entrance. But the cunning Odysseus planned an escape. When the giant returned in the evening, he ate two more of Odysseus' companions. At this point Odysseus, who had brought some wine with him into the cave, offered Polyphemus a great bowl of strong wine, and then another, and so on until the giant was drunk. He lay down and slept, snoring hideously. Then Odysseus crept up to him, carrying a stake which he had sharpened during the day and hardened in the fire. He thrust the stake into Polyphemus' single eye and whirled the heated point around. The giant gave a fearful bellow, groped blindly for the entrance of the cave, and sat down, so that, even though they had blinded him, Odysseus and his companions could not escape. However, Odysseus had a plan: he lashed the sheep together in threes, so that the middle sheep of each set of three would support one man holding on underneath the animal; Odysseus himself clung to the underside of the ram. So, in the morning they were able to leave the cave in this way, for though the blinded giant felt along the backs of the sheep, he did not discover the men beneath.

This was merely the beginning of Odysseus' troubles. The giant Polyphemus was a son of Poseidon, the god of the sea, and he prayed to Poseidon to make Odysseus' journey a hazardous one. And so, indeed, it was.

One of the places they had to pass was the island of the Sirens, strange birdlike creatures whose beautiful singing bewitched anyone who heard it. To guard against this, Odysseus told his men to tie him to the ship's mast, and he gave them lumps of wax to put into their ears so that they would not hear the magical song of the Sirens. Sure enough, when they came near the island, and the Sirens sang their enchanting song, even Odysseus felt his wits leave him. He struggled to free himself, calling on his men to release him and to unplug their ears. Luckily, they had carried out his earlier orders, so they ignored his frenzied commands, tied him all the tighter and rowed safely past the island.

The next danger was in the narrow sea between Italy and Sicily, for on one side of the sea passage was the fearsome whirlpool of Charybdis and on the other side stood the cave of the dreadful monster Scylla. She had twelve feet and six necks with a head on each, and in each of her heads were three gruesome mouths. Odysseus steered well away from Charybdis but as the ship was passing

Scylla's cave, she appeared and grabbed six men. While she feasted on those, Odysseus and the rest of his men managed to escape.

Odysseus had many more adventures before he reached his home in Ithaca. He lost all of his men when Zeus hurled a thunderbolt at his ship to punish his men for killing some of the sacred cattle of Helios. Odysseus himself was nearly sucked into the whirlpool of Charybdis and drowned. Eventually he landed on the magic island of Ogygia, where the nymph Calypso kept him for seven long years. He longed for his home and his wife Penelope. At last, the goddess Athena pleaded on his behalf, and he was allowed to build a raft and make his way back to Ithaca.

His troubles were not over yet, for he discovered that his wife Penelope was surrounded by 108 suitors who were living off his food and wine. Each of them had been plaguing Penelope for three years to marry him. They said that Odysseus was dead and would not return. But she had remained faithful to him and tricked the suitors by telling them that before she married anyone, she must finish weaving a fine robe which would be the shroud of Odysseus' father Laertes. By day she wove, and by night she crept back to her work and unraveled the cloth she had made. In this way, she had kept the suitors waiting. Now they had discovered her trick and intended to force Penelope to choose one of them as her husband the very day after Odysseus, unknown to the people of Ithaca, had at last reached home.

All this was told to Odysseus by the goddess Athena, who also gave him some advice as to how he might outwit the band of powerful suitors, although he was but one against so many. Then she sent to Pylos and made sure that Telemachus, who was the son of Odysseus and now grown into a fine young man, came safely home to Ithaca. With Telemachus, Odysseus made plans to defeat the suitors. Penelope had arranged for a contest to be held the following day in the great hall with herself as the winner's prize. The suitors' task was to string the bow of Odysseus and shoot arrows through twelve axes set upright in the floor. It was arranged that Telemachus would remove all the weapons on the walls of the hall but let the contest take place as planned.

Next morning Odysseus went to his palace disguised as a beggar. No one recognized him – no one, that is, except his old hound Argus. The suitors had kicked the dog out of the palace to die in the dirt. Blind and dying, he still recognized Odysseus after all those years, struggled feebly to his feet, and tried to wag his tail. Then he died. Odysseus was immensely moved by the faithfulness of his old friend.

In the hall, the wooers were unable even to string the great bow of Odysseus. After all had failed, Odysseus, still disguised as a beggar, asked if he might try. Penelope permitted this: perhaps a strange feeling within her told her that this man would bring her good fortune.

Odysseus strung his great bow and shot the arrows through each of the axe handles. Then, he and Telemachus turned their attention on the suitors. There was a swift and terrible slaughter. The suitors had few weapons with which to defend themselves and the hall's doors were locked. Soon the floor was red with blood.

Thus it was that, after twenty years of great trials and tribulations, Odysseus and Penelope were reunited. The oracle's warning to Odysseus had come true, but now at last the troubles that had begun with the Trojan war were concluded and peace reigned once more.

III The end of Homer's world
The decline of Mycenae

Though it cannot be proved that the Trojan war actually happened, there is some archaeological evidence to support Homer's story. One of the settlements on the site of Troy, which Schliemann began to excavate in 1870, seems to have been destroyed by an enemy during the period in question. The remains show that the Trojans had not only improved their fortifications, but had made preparations to withstand a long siege, improving their water supply and cutting storage pits into the floors of their houses.

After the war, the Mycenaean civilization flourished for a long time, but eventually, like every other great civilization, it collapsed. Maybe the long and exhausting war against Troy, which had kept the Mycenaean leaders away from their homes for ten years, undermined the structure of this first great Greek civilization. The stories of the homecomings of Agamemnon and Odysseus certainly show that the government had become weak in their lands. While the great leaders were away, smaller men must have seized what power they could. However, another threat arose.

In the thirteenth century B.C., a people known as the Dorians began a series of attacks on the northern edges of the Mycenaean world. Gradually these attacks became bolder, and even-

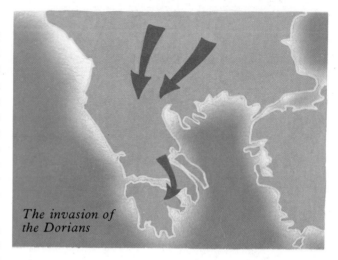

The invasion of the Dorians

tually this barbarous and fierce people swept down into Greece through Macedonia and Thessaly. They came in great hordes and there was no possibility of making peace with them, for they were desperate for land and food. They were themselves being harassed by other tribes.

It seems strange to us that the great fortresses of Mycenae, Tiryns, and Pylos, with their mighty walls, were unable to withstand these barbarians who had less developed fighting skills and smaller supplies of weapons. Perhaps too much success had made the Mycenaeans soft and easy-going, and, quarreling among themselves, they could not

Mycenae as it is today

agree on a common plan to defeat the invaders. We cannot be certain what happened, but we do have archaeological evidence to show that one by one the great fortresses fell and were destroyed by fire. Mycenae held out somewhat longer than the others, possibly because of its commanding position in the hills, but eventually, about 1100 B.C., it fell.

The Greeks made up a legend that the Dorian invaders were the sons of Heracles, a famous Greek hero who had performed many labors. He had been exiled from Mycenae, and its people came to believe that the Dorians were his sons, returning to claim their territory.

What happened to the Mycenaeans who survived the savagery of the invading hordes? Many of them must have been slaughtered in the destruction of the fortresses. Some undoubtedly became the slaves of the Dorians. Those that were left fled by land and sea, some to the islands of the Mediterranean, such as Cyprus, others to join in the great force which attacked Egypt during the reign of Ramses III. This was a strange time of disturbance and movement of peoples in the lands around the Mediterranean, and much of what happened is not clear. However, among the leaders of the force that Ramses defeated are names which could be Mycenaean. Those that did not go abroad fled into the mountains of Arcadia, in the western part of the Peloponnesus. The language spoken there in later times is supposed to have been similar to the Mycenaean language.

The golden age of Greece

After the collapse of the Mycenaean civilization, Greece went into a decline which lasted several hundred years, a period known as the Dark Age, for the lights of civilization seemed to go out. Standards of living declined, for the Dorians were a primitive people who lived in poor settlements and used only the crudest implements and weapons. They did not build great cities and tombs as the Mycenaeans had done, and they left behind them no writings of any sort. The idea of any kind of central government was also lost. During the period of Mycenaean rule, it had been relatively easy and safe to travel across Greece, at least within the Mycenaean Empire. In the Dark Age, however, roads were overrun, the population shrank, people lived in small communities, and brigands roamed freely through the land.

Slowly, the Dorians must have learned the arts and skills of civilized life. Gradually their pottery, known as "geometric," improved in its quality, and more elegant shapes and designs were developed. In the eighth century B.C., the Dorians learned the Phoenician alphabet and adapted it so that they could write their own language. Thus the ancient language of the Minoans and Mycenaeans, after many changes, came to be written down in the form that we know as ancient Greek. Many words and elements of that language survive in most European tongues.

When Greece emerged from the Dark Age in the eighth century, it was divided into a number of city-states, each existing somewhat like the separate countries of today. Though the people all spoke Greek, each city-state had its own separate dialect, its own customs, its own laws, its own political system, and, of course, its own army. The most important city-states were Athens, Sparta, Corinth, Megara, and Thebes.

Over the next five hundred years (750–250 B.C.) these cities developed a culture far more refined and glorious than anything that the world had seen before. The Mycenaean civilization had glorified the arts of war and fighting, but in the Greece of this period, and especially in Athens, men refined the arts of peaceful living in communities. Athens was the center of this new civilization, one which has influenced life in the Western world to this day.

One of the reasons that Athens became so

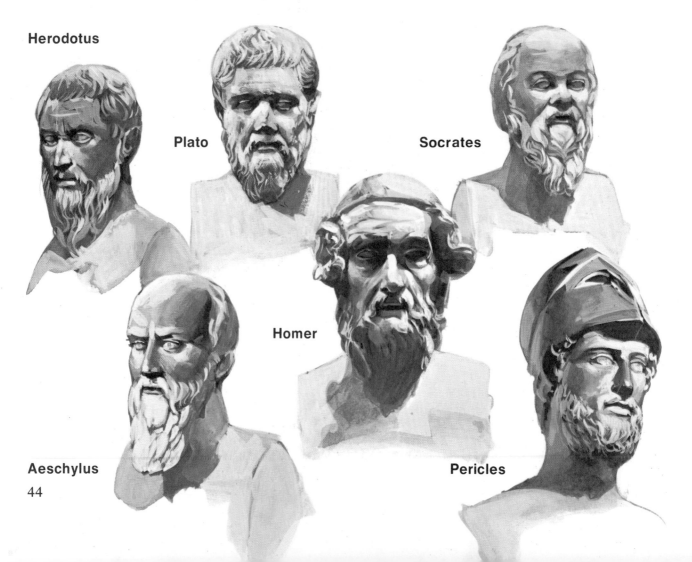

Herodotus

Plato

Socrates

Homer

Aeschylus

Pericles

44

powerful was its navy. The Athenian navy was larger than that of any other Greek community, and with it the Athenians built up an empire which extended all over the Aegean. However, they were cunning and did not call it an empire. Instead, they called it an alliance, and said that all they were doing was protecting their "allies" from the Persians. Every year, from all over the Aegean, money was sent by their allies to the Athenians. With this great tribute, the city grew ever richer and more able to build magnificent temples and other buildings and to support every form of civilized life. The beginning of Athenian success was perhaps the battle of Marathon in 480 B.C. The Persians had been pressing further into Greece. Athens asked Sparta for aid against the Persians, but the Spartans refused, so the Athenians went into battle alone and won a great victory. So began their finest and most confident period. It was around this time that literature, art, and architecture flourished most vigorously in Athens.

If you go to Athens today, you can still see on the Acropolis – the great rock which was the heart and citadel of the ancient city – the magnificent temples which the Athenians built to their gods. Chief among them was Athena, supposed to have founded Athens and to be the ever-watchful protectress of the city. Every four years, the Athenians held a festival in honor of Athena. They erected a mighty statue to the goddess which was 29.7 feet (nine meters) high and made of solid gold and ivory. This stood in the Parthenon, the finest and largest temple on the Acropolis. On the day of the festival, a procession of all the freemen of Athens walked up to the Acropolis from the agora in the lower city in order to present the image of the goddess with a new tunic. The statues and carvings from the Parthenon show us what this procession looked like. These statues and carvings also show us that the Athenians never spared any expense or any labor in their attempts to create the most perfect and ideal view of what men and women could be like.

In every way, the Greeks of the fifth century B.C. attempted to achieve excellence and perfection in their way of life and in their works of art. Their sculptures of men and women are full of grace and beauty. They had great skill in measurement, calculation, and building. Their pottery was so fine that they became the sole suppliers of high-grade pottery in the Mediterranean world. They produced great thinkers: philosophers such as Socrates and Plato would sit for hours in the public places of the city discussing subjects such as justice and truth. The Athenian writer

The Acropolis in Athens as it is today.

Herodotus was the first man to write a history book. These Greek philosophers have influenced the thinking of the Western world ever since.

Furthermore, Athens has influenced the way we organize our countries, for she was the founder of democracy. Every Athenian, provided he was freeborn and male, had the right to speak in the democratic assembly of the agora and the right to vote. Instead of a king or emperor making all the decisions, the people ruled themselves under the guidance of such great statesmen as Pericles.

Throughout this later Greek civilization, the mighty deeds of the heroes of Mycenae and Troy were not forgotten. The poet Homer, who had probably written the *Iliad* and *Odyssey* about 800 B.C., was widely read and greatly praised. Later writers, such as Aeschylus, who himself fought in the battle of Marathon, took up the old stories of Agamemnon and the other heroes and rewrote them to appeal to the Athenians in particular. Fifth-century Athens looked back to the days of Mycenae and Troy as a golden age when men were larger than life and when the gods involved themselves in the lives of men.

When, in 323 B.C., Alexander the Great of Macedonia conquered Greece and then proceeded to unify the known world, he made possible the spread of Greek culture and ideas throughout Europe. So it was that stories of the ancient Mycenaeans and Trojans have come to be a part of our lives. So, too, archaeologists such as Heinrich Schliemann were inspired to search the ancient sites and to prove that – whether or not the great heroes actually lived – a powerful Mycenaean civilization certainly existed.